DR XARGLE'S
BOOK OF
EARTH HOUNDS

A Red Fox Book

Published by Random Century Children's Books
20 Vauxhall Bridge Road, London SW1V 2SA
A division of the Random Century Group

London Melbourne Sydney Auckland
Johannesburg and agencies throughout the world

First published by Andersen Press Limited 1989
Red Fox edition 1991

Printed in Italy by Grafiche AZ, Verona.

ISBN 0 09 964020 1

DR XARGLE'S
BOOK OF
EARTH HOUNDS

Translated into Human by Jeanne Willis
Pictures by Tony Ross

Red Fox

Good morning, class.

Today we are going to learn about Earth Hounds.

Earth Hounds have fangs at the front and a waggler
at the back.

To find out which is which, hold a sausage at both
ends.

Earth Hounds have buttons for eyes, a sniffer with two holes in and a long, pink flannel.

With the pink flannel they lick their
undercarriages,

frogs which are deceased and the icicles of
Earthlets who are not looking.

Earth Hounds can stand on four legs, three legs and two legs. They can jump as high as a roast beef.

For dinner they consume jellymeat, skeleton biscuits, a fairy cake,

a portion of best carpet and a sock that is four
days old.

After this feast they must be taken to a place called walkies, which has many lamp-posts.

The Earth Hound is attached to a string so that he can be pulled along in the sitting position.

In the park, the Earthling gathers a stick from a tree
and hurls it all around.
The Earth Hound is made to fetch it.

Then the Earthling takes a bouncing sphere and flings it in the pond.

This time the Earthling has to fetch it.

On the way home, the Earth Hound rolls in the pat of a moohorn.

He arrives back at the Earth Dwelling with stinkfur and hides under the duvet of the Earthling.

Here are some phrases I want you to learn:
"Where is Rover?"
"Is something wrong with the drains?"
"Either he goes or I do!"

Earth Hounds hate the bath of bubbles. They tuck their wagglers between their legs and make a Wooo-Woooooo noise.

Once clean they dry themselves on heaps of compost.

Here is a baby Earth Hound, or Houndlet, asleep in the nocturnal footwear of an Earthling.

On the floor the Earthling has placed many
newspapers for the Houndlet to read.

That is the end of today's lesson.

If you are all good and quiet, we will visit Planet
Earth to play with a real Houndlet.

Those of you who want to bring your own pets along, please sit at the back of the spaceship.

Other titles in the Red Fox picture book series (incorporating Beaver Books)

Not Like That, Like This Tony Bradman and Debbie Van Der Beek
If At First You Do Not See Ruth Brown
I Don't Like It Ruth Brown
John Patrick Norman McHennessy, The Boy Who Was Always Late John Burningham
Granpa (the book of the film) John Burningham
The Cross With Us Rhinoceros John Bush and Paul Geraghty
The Last Dodo Ann and Reg Cartwright
Ellie's Doorstep Alison Catley
Herbie the Dancing Hippo Charlotte Van Emst
Ben's Baby Michael Foreman
Over the Steamy Swamp Paul Geraghty
Old Bear Jane Hissey
Little Bear's Trousers Jane Hissey
Little Bear Lost Jane Hissey
The Big Alfie and Annie Rose Storybook Shirley Hughes
Jake Deborah King
When Sheep Cannot Sleep Satoshi Kitamura
Albert and Albertine Colin and Moira Maclean
Albert and Albertine at the Seaside Colin and Moira Maclean

Not Now, Bernard David McKee
The Sad Story of Veronica Who Played the Violin David McKee
The Snow Woman David McKee
Who's a Clever Baby, Then? David McKee
We Can Say No! David Pithers and Sarah Greene
A Day of Rhymes Sarah Pooley
Stories for Summer Alf Prøysen
Stories for Christmas Alf Prøysen
Mrs Pepperpot's Christmas Alf Prøysen
Bad Mood Bear John Richardson
Stone Soup Tony Ross
The Three Pigs Tony Ross
Carry Go Bring Come Vyanne Samuels and Jennifer Northway
A Witch Got On At Paddington Station Dyan Sheldon and Wendy Smith
The Monster Bed Jeanne Willis and Susan Varley
Dr Xargle's Book of Earthlets Jeanne Willis and Tony Ross
The Tale of Georgie Grub Jeanne Willis and Margaret Chamberlain
Maggie and the Monster Elizabeth Winthrop and Tomie de Paola